The Great Penne Pasta Odyssey

Narrated by Jordan Gupta and Veer-Raj Gupta

Written by Ashish Gupta

Dedication

To my daughter, Jordan and son, Veer-Raj, who invented a brilliant dinnertime game called "The Question Game" to satisfy their daily curiosity.

The Great Penne Pasta Odyssey

"Dinner's ready, kiddos!" Mom calls out, searching the house for hungry faces. "Jo, where's your brother? Can you give him a shout?"

Jo, ever curious about the meal, asks, "What did you make, Mom?"

"Your favourite - penne pasta!" Mom replies with a smile.

Jo's eyes light up. "Yum! No need to hunt for Vee," she says mischievously. "Just a whiff of penne pasta and he'll come out of hiding faster than a shooting star!"

Grinning, Jo calls out, "Vee, Mama made penne pasta! Come on over, and we can play the question game!"

"Penne pasta?!" A shout comes from upstairs. "Coming right over!"

Moments later, Vee bursts into the room, ready for dinner and a game.

Jo - "Do I look like a **Saber-toothed** tiger?"
Vee - "More like a **Saber-toothed** cat."

Did you know the word "saber" comes from the French word "sabre," meaning a heavy curved sword? Saber-toothed tigers lived up to their name with two long,sharp canine teeth that acted like built-in swords!

Sadly, these awesome hunters couldn't handle the freezing temperatures of the last ice age and went extinct around 12,000 years ago.

Vee - "I can even see Mickey and Minney on your ear ring with my new **binoculars**!"

Jo - "Your **binoculars** are melting away, little explorer!"

The word "binoculars" combines two Latin words: "bīnus" meaning "double" and "oculus" meaning "eye." So unlike telescopes, binoculars allow you to see with both eyes at the same time!
On a clear night, you can spot the Orion Nebula, Mars, Saturn, Jupiter, and even some satellites using a regular pair of binoculars.

Jo - "This whistle is so cool, only if it could work too."
Vee - "yeah and if it did, i would use this whistle to wake you up everyday."

The first man-made whistles were carved from tree branches and gourds. Any guesses why?

Vee - "My **fingers** are so big, they can almost tickle your nose."
Jo - "Bring your delicious **fingers** closer, I love to take a bite."

Bend your middle finger and put your hand flat on the table.
Lift your thumb, index finger, and pinkie. Pretty simple, right?
Now, try lifting your ring finger.

It doesn't budge, does it? That's because it shares a muscle with your
pinkie and middle fingers, so it can't move independently.
Fun, isn't it?

Jo - "I will color my entire color book collection with these **crayons**. Each one of them will be a masterpiece."
Vee - "And I will use the **crayons** to camouflage myself during hide-and-seek with Mom!"

Did you know the word "crayon" has a chalky past?
It comes from the French word "craie," which itself comes from the
Latin word "creta." Both these words mean "chalk"!

Vee - "This teeny tiny **straw** is so neat! It's coming with me on every treat!"
Jo - "This **straw** will not last too long, when you are eating it and drinking with it at the same time."

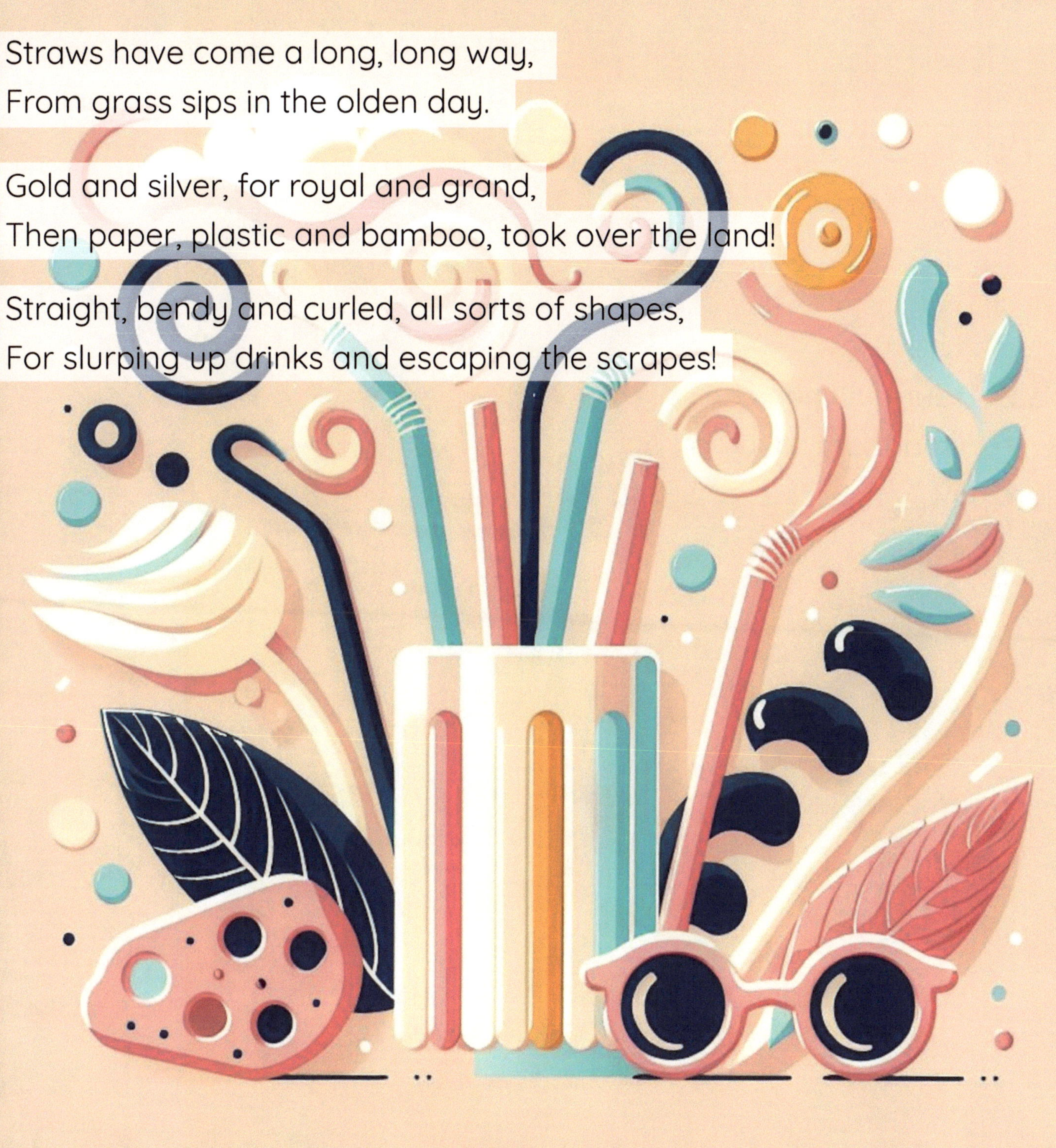

Straws have come a long, long way,
From grass sips in the olden day.

Gold and silver, for royal and grand,
Then paper, plastic and bamboo, took over the land!

Straight, bendy and curled, all sorts of shapes,
For slurping up drinks and escaping the scrapes!

Jo - "Fun fact! Penne comes from 'penna,' which means feather – like a quill pen!"
Vee - "Your quill pen can only write in marinara sauce ink right now."

Feather pens for 1,200 years! Yep, knights and pirates wrote with sharpened FEATHERS for centuries!

Even the super important stuff like the Magna Carta and the Declaration of Independence was written using a quill pen!

Vee - "My **telescope** is so powerful, I can see everything on the moon! Like it's right next door!"
Jo - "Whoa there, little explorer! Let's see how many craters your super-powered **telescope** can spot on the moon tonight! Think you can find the big one Tycho?"

Did you know the word "telescope" comes from Greek words? "Tele" means 'far' and "skopos" means 'see,' so literally 'far-seeing'.

Telescopes are like super spy gadgets with amazing eyes! They can see stars and galaxies billions of light-years away. That means the light we see left those places billions of years ago!

So, in a way, telescopes are like time machines, letting us see the universe as it was billions of years in the past. How cool is that?

Jo - "These teeny tiny tunnels are just perfect! Choo - choo, our teeny tiny train is going to have the most magical journey ever!"
Vee - "And colorful too! Like a rainbow tunnel party. These are the absolute best tunnels ever!"

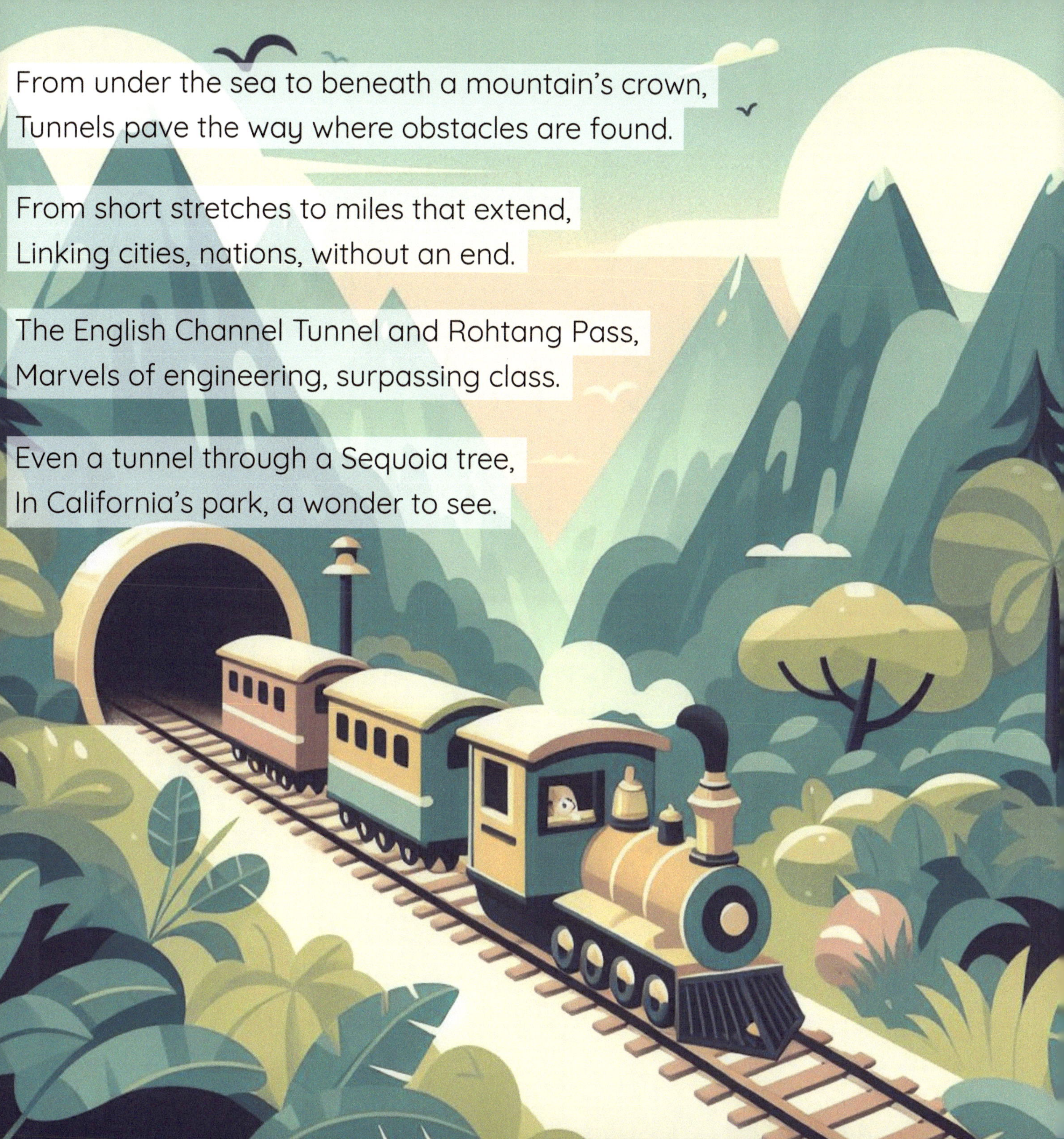

From under the sea to beneath a mountain's crown,
Tunnels pave the way where obstacles are found.

From short stretches to miles that extend,
Linking cities, nations, without an end.

The English Channel Tunnel and Rohtang Pass,
Marvels of engineering, surpassing class.

Even a tunnel through a Sequoia tree,
In California's park, a wonder to see.

Vee - "This **cannon** can shoot cannonballs farther than you can splash in the pool!"
Jo - "Oh please. Your **cannon** only shoots cheese puffs – delicious cheese puffs, but still, just cheese puffs!"

Did you know the word "cannon" has a surprisingly tubular history? It all goes back to the word "canna" in Latin, which itself comes from the Greek word "kanna."
Even further back, the ancient Mesopotamian language Akkadian used the word "qanu" – and guess what? They all mean "tube"!

Jo - "What should I play for you on my **flute**? 'Old Macdonald' or 'Mary had a little lamb'?"
Vee - "Ooh, how about you make up a new song? Like I have the best brother in the whole wide world, whole wild world, The whole wild world."
Jo - "More like - I have the most silly brother in this world."

Did you know the word "flute" comes from the Latin word flatus, meaning "to blow"?

And guess what? A flute-playing musician has so many names – they're like musical superheroes! They can be called a flute player, a flutist, a flautist, a fluter, a flutenist, or even a flutomater!

Vee - "Wow, we made so many cool things with penne pasta! I wonder what we could make with spaghetti?"
Jo - "I like the way you think! Let's ask Mom to make spaghetti for dinner tomorrow and find out!"
Vee - "You're on! Let's be spaghetti explorers!"

About the Author

Ashish Gupta is an aspiring children's book writer, or one might say, a translator of the stories lived and narrated by his two kids. Believing in the adage that 'books are your best friends,' reading and narrating stories became a cherished ritual in his household. Inspired by this, Ashish writes about the simplest pleasures of life: travel tales and the time he enjoys with his lovely wife, daughter, and son.

In another aspect of his life, Ashish holds an MBA in Finance and works as a Financial Technology Advisor in one of the Big 4 firms in Houston, Texas, USA.

Other adventures from @jovee_diaries

In "Jo and Vee's Grand Adventure", readers are invited to join two young siblings, Jo and Vee, on an unforgettable journey of exploration and discovery. From the bustling streets of their hometown to the serene landscapes of distant mountains, the duo embarks on a series of escapades that will ignite their sense of wonder and leave them with memories to last a lifetime.

Through their escapades, Jo and Vee remind us all to embrace life's adventures with open arms and to cherish the moments we share with the ones we love.